Ring-a-ding-ding

Simple ideas for tuned percussion in the classroom

By Jane Sebba

Illustrated by Alison Dexter

A & C Black • London

First published 1997
A & C Black (Publishers) Ltd
35 Bedford Row London WC1R 4JH
© 1997 A & C Black (Publishers) Ltd

Book/cassette pack ISBN 0-7136-4423-0
Book/CD pack ISBN 0-7136-4616-0

Written by Jane Sebba
Text © 1997 A & C Black
Artwork © Alison Dexter
Edited by Ana Sanderson
Designed by Dorothy Moir
Printed in Great Britain by Lavenham Press Ltd,
Suffolk

Recording presented by Jonathan Trueman.
Songs performed by Helen Speirs. Instrumental
parts, speaking and sound effects performed by
Helen Speirs, Jane Sebba and Ana Sanderson.
Recorded and mastered by Darren Nicholls.
65 minutes playing time.

Contents

About this book   4

Tuned percussion instruments   6

MUSICAL GAMES

High, middle, low   8
Track 1

Buns cross hot   10
Track 2

Ways to play   12
Track 3

Simon says   14
Track 4

Tea time   16
Track 5

Adding accidentals   18
Track 6

Announcements   20
Track 7

A's for apricot   22
Track 8

OSTINATO ACCOMPANIMENTS

Help with ostinato
accompaniments 24

Wallabies and wombats 26
Track 9

Bonfire's burning 28
Track 10

Push, push, push your bike 30
Track 11

Kookaburra 32
Track 12

A sailor went to sea 34
Track 13

Swing low, sweet chariot 36
Track 14

Mango walk 38
Track 15

Old MacDonald had a glockenspiel 40
Track 16

PENTATONIC SCALE ACTIVITIES

Pentatonic scales 42

Which notes are these? 44
Track 17

You can't go wrong 46
Track 18

My own tune 48
Track 19

What's today? 50
Track 20

Secrets of the animal kingdom 52
Track 21

Apple, apple, blackberry, apple 54
Track 22

Knock, knock! 56
Track 23

From poem to song 58
Track 24

Melody lines 60-63
Glossary and acknowledgements 64

About this book

We have all yet to meet a child who hasn't been instantly intrigued and delighted by a classroom glockenspiel. The instrument is child-sized and easy to handle, a pleasing sound can be produced immediately, and its versatility ensures that no-one gets bored.

However, the task for the teacher of organising several children at once to participate in a tuned percussion activity can be daunting – often leading the teacher to feel despondent about tuned percussion and how to use it in the classroom. The purpose of **Ring-a-ding-ding** is to make playing tuned percussion instruments instantly accessible. Without reading a note of music, you can give your children a tuneful and educational musical experience which both you and they will enjoy.

All children sing, some more tunefully than others, but whatever their vocal skills, they cannot see the mechanism which creates the sound. However, tuned percussion instruments, with note-bars arranged so neatly and satisfactorily, provide us with a perfect visual aid for teaching our children about pitch in music. With the name of the note marked on each bar, and the size and position of each note clearly visible, even children who find abstract concepts hard to grasp will understand the principles of high and low.

Finding your way around the book and recording

There are three sections in the book: **musical games** (pages 8 – 23), **ostinato accompaniments** to songs (pages 24 – 41) and **pentatonic scale activities** for making up music (pages 42 – 59).

The items in each section progress from easy to more difficult. You can work through a section to give your children the opportunity to accumulate musical skills; alternatively, you can pick and choose items suitable for your children. Some items can be used as quick warming-up activities, while others can last for one or more lessons.

All the activities can take place in the classroom. Many take into consideration limited resources and require only one instrument. Others give ideas for using more instruments if you have them.

The accompanying recording takes you step-by-step through all the activities, giving you the opportunity to hear how the musical games might progress, how the songs and their accompanying ostinatos sound, and example musical ideas that might result from the starting points for making up music in the pentatonic scale activities section. If you are a confident musician, this book will provide you with a wealth of new ideas; if you are not, it will guide you gently into practical music-making.

Classroom music-making

Your music lessons incorporating percussion instruments will be enjoyable and productive if both you and your children observe the following points.

Successful music–making is often a product of good team–work.
Just as football players must be aware of the other members of the team, so must musicians be aware of and listen to others in order to play

together as a team. Listening to others is a skill in its own right and some children will find it difficult at first. Point out that playing a musical piece is not a race or competition to win or to be the first to finish.

Establish some ground rules for when to be silent.
When you give a child a percussion instrument, (s)he will want to play it – and the effect is often noisy! It is very difficult to give instructions for a musical performance when several children are playing percussion instruments, so it is advisable to make a rule that instruments and beaters should be placed on the floor or a table when not in use.

Silence is an important component of music. Encourage the performers to be still like statues at the beginning and at the end of their pieces. Listeners should always be quiet while others perform – and performers should give their audience something worth being quiet for!

For each item in this book which includes a song, starting notes for the tune are given.
When combining singing with tuned percussion, it is important to begin singing on the correct note.

To find your starting note, you can either familiarise yourself with the recording, or you can play the first note given in the **teacher's help box** on a tuned percussion instrument, and then reproduce it vocally. The **teacher's help box** below shows a song beginning on the note **F**.

The alto xylophone is closest in range to children's voices, so if you have one, use it for giving starting notes. If you find it difficult to reproduce notes vocally, delegate the job to someone in your class for whom it is easy.

For each item which includes a song or a chant, a pulse should be established so that everyone performs at the same speed.
Again, you can either take the pulse from the relevant track on the recording. Alternatively, you can look at the count-in given in the **teacher's help box**, take a moment to establish the speed of the song or chant in your head, then count aloud to bring everyone in together. Tell the children beforehand what you are going to count and when they should start singing. The **teacher's help boxes** below show a song and a chant, both with four beat count-ins. The circles above the words of the chant indicate the pulse.

Teacher's help box:
showing count-in and first notes of the song

1	2	3	4	F F	D C
				Which notes	are these?

Teacher's help box:
showing count-in and pulse of the chant

1	2	3	4	•	•	•	•
				High,	mid-dle,	low	

Tuned percussion instruments

The tuned percussion instruments referred to in this book are the most commonly used ones – xylophones, glockenspiels, metallophones and chime bars. When the note-bars of these instruments are struck, a definite pitch or note (such as **A**, **B** or **C** and so on) is heard. By contrast, untuned percussion instruments (such as tambourines, drums and cymbals) produce sounds which have no definite pitch. On a tuned instrument, you can literally play a tune. Try playing the beginning of *Frère Jacques* – **C D E C C D E C**.

Recognising different tuned percussion instruments

In Greek, *xulon* means wood, and *phonos* means sound, giving us the word xylophone. Xylophones have wooden bars which rest on a deep resonator box which helps to amplify the sound.

In German, *glocken* means bell, and *spiel* means play, giving us the word glockenspiel. Glockenspiels have shiny metal bars which are usually thin and narrow. They are often black and white, as on a piano. The sound of the glockenspiel is bell-like.

Metallophones also have metal bars, but they are thicker and wider than those of the glockenspiel. They are made of a metal alloy with a matt finish. Like the xylophone, the bars rest on a deep resonator box.

A chime bar is a single bar, made out of wood, fibre or metal, mounted on its own small resonating box. Each chime bar can sound one note only. Chime bars can be purchased individually, or as whole sets - a set can be played in the same way as a xylophone, glockenspiel, or metallophone.

Family members

Glockenspiels, xylophones, metallophones and chime bar sets are available in different sizes. The smallest instruments produce the highest notes and are called soprano instruments; the largest in size produce the lowest sounds and are called bass (pronounced base) instruments; the instruments in between, both in size and sound, are the alto instruments.

The notes and their names

Most instruments will have at least one row of twelve note-bars. Place the instrument with the longest bar which produces the lowest note to the player's left. The shortest bar which produces the highest note should be to the player's right, so that from left to right, the sound of the instrument gets higher.

The musical note names – **A B C D E F G** – are the first seven letters of the alphabet. There is no H; after **G**, the sequence of letters repeats. The result is that there are several notes of the same name related to each other by their sound as well as their name. If you play a high **D** and a low **D**, you will hear that they are the 'same' note. In this book, high notes, such as high **D** are shown as **D'**.

Diatonic and chromatic instruments – sharps and flats

Diatonic tuned percussion instruments have only one row of notes which correspond to the white notes on a piano. A chromatic tuned percussion instrument has a second row of notes which corresponds to the black notes on a piano. These are the sharp (♯) and flat (♭) notes. A sharp note sounds a little higher than its namesake, (**F♯** is higher than **F**) and a flat note sounds a little lower, (**G♭** is lower than **G**). Each note on the second row of the instrument has two names – one sharp and one flat. **G♭** and **F♯** are the same note. Each note on the second row is generally labelled with its more commonly used name. **F♯** is more commonly referred to than **G♭**.

Beaters
There are many different types of beaters; hard (wood or plastic), medium-hard (rubber or medium-hard plastic), hard felt and soft felt. Beaters can also differ in size and weight; a better sound quality can be achieved with heavier beaters. The sounds produced on tuned percussion instruments will vary according to the type of beaters used to play them. Children will enjoy experimenting with hard and soft heads on all the instruments. Any beater can be used to play any instrument, with the exception of hard beaters on metallophones, as they can damage the metal alloy.

Holding beaters and space to play
If you have sufficient beaters, give each child a pair of identical beaters, one to hold in each hand. Your children will probably prefer to use their dominant hand, but encourage them to alternate their hands.

The note-bar should be struck with the round head of the beater. The other end should be held in the palm of the hand, with the fingers lightly wrapped around the stick and the back of the hand facing up. The beater should not be held as though it were a pencil. The wrist must be flexible, to enable the head of the beater to bounce gently off the bar. Some children may need frequent reminders about how to hold the beater.

To achieve a good sound quality from a tuned percussion instrument, the head of the beater should 'bounce' off the bar. The children can imagine that the head of the beater is a ball, and bounce it gently off the centre of the bar, between the two rows of pins. This enables the bar to vibrate freely, and allows the instrument to resonate. If the head of the beater remains on the bar, the vibration is dampened, and the sound will 'die'. Some children find this action difficult and will need to practise.

Make sure each player has plenty of space. Ideally, instruments should be at a child's waist level on a table so that the children can stand to play. If instruments are placed on the floor, encourage the children to kneel to play so that their arm movements are not restricted.

Making tuned percussion parts easier to play
To help children see which note-bars they should be using for a particular activity or song, you can either highlight the note-bars by placing stickers on them, or remove those not being used. Bars on xylophones, glockenspiels and metallophones can be removed easily – simply ensure that they are lifted off the instrument with both hands. (Never lever them up at one end.) Always replace all bars correctly after a session.

For more information about classroom percussion instruments, see *Agogo bells to Xylophone* (more information on back cover).

High, middle, low,
These are notes we know.
Choose your cards and then you play,
Make a tune today.

This game familiarises children with low, middle and high sounds. Using the notes (low) **C**, (middle) **G** and (high) **C'**, a child plays a short tune which the other children identify.

high

middle

low

The material above is photocopiable for the teaching purposes specified in this book.

You will need:
• these notes
• twelve cards (four **high**, four **middle** and four **low**) made with photocopies of the pictures above.

1	2	3	4	•	•	•	•
				High,	mid-dle,	low	

The game

1. Prepare for the game.
The children sit in a circle, if possible. The instrument is placed in the centre of the circle, or somewhere accessible. Shuffle the cards and lay them out face down near the instrument.

2. The children perform the chant.
As they do this, they pass the beater around the circle.

3. A child plays a tune.
The child holding the beater on the last word of the chant turns over four cards and plays the corresponding pattern of notes.

4. The children sing the tune.
They do this using the words **high**, **middle** and **low** and show the relative position of each note with their hands.

Variations
- The child with the beater turns over six cards.
- The child with the beater plays a tune, then extends it by playing it backwards.
- Use other relatively high, middle and low notes, such as (low) **A**, (middle) **E** and (high) **C'**.
- The children in the circle cover their eyes and identify the sequence of notes by listening only.

(First version)
High, low, middle.
High, low, middle.
Change the order of the notes from
High, low, middle.

(Second version)
High, low, middle.
High, low, middle.
Change the order of the notes to
Middle, low, high.

The children sing the first version of this song to the tune of *Hot cross buns*. The first three notes in the tune are (high) **C'**, (low) **C** and (middle) **F**, and these notes are used in the game.

A child chooses a new sequence for the three notes which is then used for a new version of the song.

You will need:
• these notes.

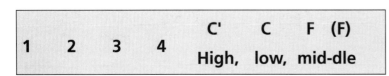

1	2	3	4	C'	C	F	(F)
				High,	low,	mid-dle	

The game

1. Prepare for the game.

Point out to the children that the words **high**, **low** and **middle** correspond to the pitch of the notes in the song.

2. The children sing the song.

One child sits by the instrument holding the beaters as the others sing the song.

3. The child at the instrument plays a new tune.

At the end of the song, the child makes up a new tune by playing the three notes in a new order. (S)he identifies the notes of the new tune using the words **low**, **middle** and **high**.

4. The children incorporate the new tune into the second version of the song.

They use the words **low**, **middle**, and **high** when singing the new tune and show the relative position of each note by with their hands.

Variations

• The children cover their eyes and identify the pitches of the new tune by listening.
• Allow the children to use the same note twice.

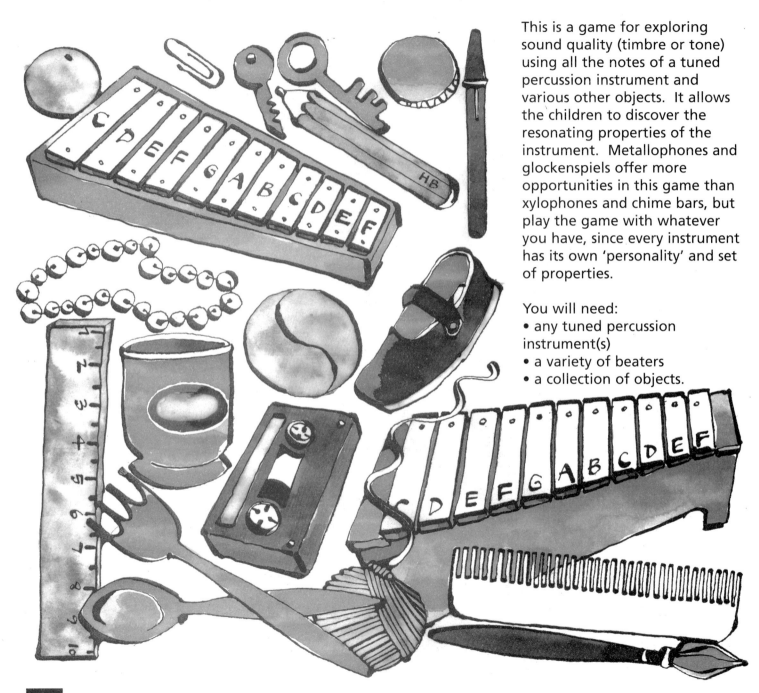

This is a game for exploring sound quality (timbre or tone) using all the notes of a tuned percussion instrument and various other objects. It allows the children to discover the resonating properties of the instrument. Metallophones and glockenspiels offer more opportunities in this game than xylophones and chime bars, but play the game with whatever you have, since every instrument has its own 'personality' and set of properties.

You will need:
• any tuned percussion instrument(s)
• a variety of beaters
• a collection of objects.

The game

1. Prepare for the game.

Position the instruments, beaters and objects so that all the children can see them.

2. The children take turns to explore ways to make sounds on the instrument.

Each child looks for original ways to play. Encourage the children to experiment and to be inventive, taking care not to damage the instruments.

Here are some ideas for making sounds:
- bounce a ping pong ball on the note-bars;
- blow over the note-bars;
- pull a comb across the edge of a note-bar;
- tap or drag fingernails or knuckles across the note-bars;
- place lentils on a note-bar and strike it gently with a beater;
- strike a note-bar with a beater, then stop the sound immediately by touching the note bar with a finger;
- strike a note-bar with a beater and touch it with a key while it is still vibrating.

Variations

- Position the instruments, objects and player behind a screen. The children who are listening then describe how they think a sound is being made.

Simon says

track 4

In this musical version of the game *Simon says*, the children respond to two notes of different pitch: (low) **D** and (high) **D'**. The first note indicates to the children to copy the leader, and the second indicates to them to remain still.

You will need:
• these notes
• a large book.

The game

1. First play **Simon says** *using the words 'do this' and 'do that'.*

Say **'do this'** and then perform an action.
The children copy the action.

Say **'do this'** and then perform an action.
The children copy the action.

Say **'do that'** and then perform an action.
The children remain still.

You can say 'do this' as many times as you like before you say 'do that'.

2. *Then play* Simon says *using the two notes.*
Position the instrument behind an open book.

Play (low) **D** and then perform an action.
The children copy the action.

Play (low) **D** and then perform an action.
The children copy the action.

Play (high) **D'** and then perform an action.
The children remain still.

Variations

- Play the game with a different pair of notes, such as **E** and **B**.
- Play the game with a pair of chords, such as **C** and **G** played together for **'do this'** and **F** and **B** played together for **'do that'**.

- Make a rule that a child who makes a mistake is out.
- Choose two children to play the part of Simon; one plays the notes and the other performs an action for the children to copy.

This game develops children's musical awareness and listening skills. One child takes the part of a whale and another takes the part of a little fish. The whale attempts to catch the little fish by listening to musical clues given by the rest of the children.

You will need:
• a blindfold
• at least four tuned percussion instruments with these notes, though you could use as many instruments as you have available.

Give various children the opportunity to be the whale and the little fish.

The game

1. Prepare for the game.
The children sit in a circle, if possible, with the two children chosen to be the little fish and the whale in the middle. The whale is blindfolded.

2. The fish slowly moves around inside the circle.
The three or four children nearest to the fish quietly say 'yum-yum'; those further away say 'swish-swish'. As the fish moves, the children change the word they say.

3. The fish chooses a place to stand still.
The children in the circle continue to say their words. The whale listens to the words to detect the position of the fish.

4. The whale tries to touch the little fish.
With outstretched arms, the whale walks carefully in the direction (s)he thinks the little fish is. If the whale manages to touch the fish before reaching the edge of the circle, (s)he chooses the next whale and fish. If not, the fish chooses.

5. Play the game again, substituting notes for the words.
Four children, placed at regular intervals around the circle, have an instrument. (Use more instruments, evenly spaced, if you have them.) The children nearest to the fish hum or play the note **A**; those furthest away hum or play the note **G**. As the fish moves around the circle, the children change their note.

Variation

• Play the game using other pairs of notes, such as **D** and **F**, or **D** and **G**.

Make a note lower, down to a flat,
Which is the number that *(clap)* does that?
1   2   3   4   5   6   7   8.

Sharpen a note and what have you done?
You've made it higher! *(clap)* Which one?
1   2   3   4   5   6   7   8.

Up to a sharp or down to a flat?
Listen and say which *(clap)* does that.
1   2   3   4   5   6   7   8.

Any note with a flat (♭) or a sharp (♯) in its name is called an accidental. In this game, the children listen to eight notes. Then they identify which one has been flattened or sharpened. A flattened note sounds a little lower (B♭ is lower than B), and a sharpened note sounds a little higher (F♯ is higher than F).

You will need:
• a tuned percussion instrument with a full complement of flats and sharps, if possible, or at least F♯ and B♭.

Give various children the opportunity to be the *accidental adder* – the one who plays the instrument.

1	2	3	4	•	•	•	•
				Make a note low - er,	down	to a	flat

The game

1. Prepare for the game.
Position the instrument so that the children cannot see it. Choose a child to play the instrument; (s)he is the accidental adder and sits at the instrument.

2. The children perform the first chant.
After the chant, the accidental adder plays eight notes at the same speed at which the numbers were spoken. The notes are all the same except for one which is flattened. The children say which note (the first, second, third, and so on) was flattened.

3. The children perform the second chant.
The accidental adder plays eight notes, all the same, except for one which is sharpened. The children identify the sharpened note.

4. The children perform the third chant.
The accidental adder can play either sharps or flats with this chant. Listeners must decide which was the note with the accidental, and whether it was a flat or a sharp.

Variation
• Play the game allowing the accidental adder to sharpen or flatten up to a maximum of three out of eight notes.

Announcements track 7

In this game, half the children are station masters and the other half are announcers. Each station master plays two patterns of notes on cue; each announcer directs steamtrain sounds made by the children.

You will need:
• these notes
• (optional) two hats, one each for the performing station master and announcer.

The game

1. Prepare for the game.
Divide the children into equal numbers of announcers and station masters. Number the children in both groups 1, 2, 3 and so on. All the children sit in one circle, if possible. The instrument and two beaters are positioned in the centre, or somewhere accessible.

Call a number. The corresponding announcer and station master go to the centre of the circle.

3. The station master performs his/her part.
(S)he plays the first pattern on the instrument, makes the announcement and then plays the second pattern.

4. The announcer calls a platform number.
This is also the number of the next pair of children.

5. The announcer directs the train sounds.
The children in the circle perform body and mouth sounds for the arriving train. The announcer controls the volume and speed of the sound as the train approaches and stops, by raising and lowering his/her hands. Then everyone lets off steam with a loud 'Shhhhhh', fading away to silence.

6. The game is repeated with the new announcer and station master.
The children whose number was called out are the new announcer and station master. They go to the centre of the circle to perform.

Variation
• The announcer substitutes something instead of the train, such as a dinosaur, a boat or a pogo stick. The children respond with appropriate sounds.

Station master's part

Announcer's part

This material is photocopiable for the teaching purposes specified in this book.

21

(Chorus)
A B C D E F G A
These are the names of the notes we play.

1 2 3 4 A's for apricot; 1 2 3 4 A A A A A
  A B C D E F G A ... *(Pass the instrument on)*

1 2 3 4 B's for brown bread; 1 2 3 4 B B B B
  A B C D E F G A ... *(Pass the instrument on)*

1 2 3 4 C's for chips; 1 2 3 4 C C C
  A B C D E F G A ... *(Pass the instrument on)*

1 2 3 4 D's for damson jam; 1 2 3 4 D D D D D
  A B C D E F G A ... *(Pass the instrument on)*

1 2 3 4 E's for egg sandwiches; 1 2 3 4 E E E E E
  A B C D E F G A ... *(Pass the instrument on)*

1 2 3 4 F's for fish fingers; 1 2 3 4 F F F F F
  A B C D E F G A ... *(Pass the instrument on)*

1 2 3 4 G's for grapefruit; 1 2 3 4 G G G G

In this game, the children think of words which belong to a category and which begin with the letter names of the notes. During a simple chant, they play the rhythm of a short phrase which includes the word on the corresponding note.

You will need:
• one instrument for each group with these notes

• photocopies of the chart opposite
• pencils.

1	2	3	4	•	•	•	•	•	•	•
				A	B	C	D	E	F	G	A

The game

1. Prepare for the game.
Divide the children into groups of seven, if possible. Give each group a photocopied chart, a pencil and an instrument.

2. The groups think of words which belong to a category and begin with A, B, C, D, E, F and G.
Suggest a category such as food and drink. Each group chooses one word for each letter and writes it on their words chart.

3. Using its seven words, each group performs its version of the chant.
The children start the chant with, for example 'A's for apricot', then one child plays the rhythm of that phrase on the note **A**:

    A A A A
   A's for a-pri-cot

The children progress on to the next letter and word. The instrument should be passed on to the next child in the group during the chorus, so that everyone has the opportunity to play a rhythm.

4. Play the game again with a different category.
The children think of words for a new category, such as places, animals, anything found in the classroom, and so on.

Words chart

Category: ....

A's for ....

B's for ....

C's for ....

D's for ....

E's for ....

F's for ....

G's for ....

This material is photocopiable for the teaching purposes specified in this book.

Help with ostinato accompaniments

Playing ostinato accompaniments to songs is a very simple and effective way to use tuned percussion and to sound good!

What is an ostinato?

An ostinato is a pattern of notes which is repeated over and over again.

In order for an ostinato to fit successfully with a song, the performer should not rush or hesitate when repeating the pattern. An ostinato should be performed in time with the beat of the music.

Some of the ostinatos are short lines or phrases taken from the songs, which makes learning them very easy indeed.

Teaching the songs

All the songs in this section are well-known and may be familiar to you and to some of your children. To perform a song with an ostinato requires you (and the children) to be aware of two musical ideas at once: the song and the ostinato. Indeed, you will need to know the song well, for there may be times when you have to come to the rescue of an ensemble which is falling apart! Ensure that both you and the children can confidently perform a song before adding an ostinato. New words have been added to some of the songs to provide a fresh interest, but if you prefer, you can sing the original words.

You may like to use the accompanying recording to teach a song to the children; alternatively, you may prefer to sing a song yourself to the children. If possible, give the children several opportunities on several days to sing the song, before the lesson when the ostinato accompaniment will be added.

In this section, the **teacher's help box** shows the count-in, the first notes of the melody, and how the ostinato fits with the first line.

Teaching the tuned ostinatos

For every tuned ostinato accompaniment in this book, there are simple stages to go through to help you teach it to children:
• Every ostinato is derived from part of the song it accompanies. This gives the children the means to learn its rhythm.
• Each ostinato has a simple body percussion pattern that fits with it. In the first four songs (pages 26 - 33) the body percussion patterns

Teacher's help box:
showing count-in, first notes and tuned ostinato

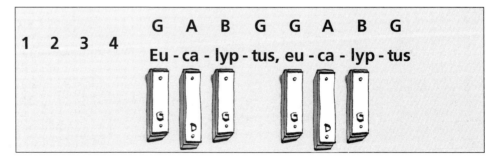

follow the high and low sounds of the ostinatos. The ostinatos of the last four songs (pages 34 - 41) are more demanding to play; for these, the body percussion prepares the child for the right and left hand beater patterns they will use to play the ostinatos.

• The body percussion easily translates into the ostinato.

• The ostinato is then simply repeated over and over again to make the accompaniment for the song.

Ending ostinato accompaniment parts
The ostinatos can be ended effectively at the same time as the song. The ostinatos for some of the songs – *Swing low, sweet chariot* (page 36), *Mango walk* (page 38) and *Old MacDonald had a glockenspiel* (page 40) – have special endings to learn which will help to make a performance sound more 'finished'.

Teaching untuned ostinato accompaniments
For most of the songs, there are suggestions of ostinato patterns to play on untuned instruments. Each of these follow the rhythm of a line or phrase from the song it accompanies, which again makes for easy learning. These parts are optional extras. To achieve a confident performance, you and the children should go through the following stages:

• Practise the untuned ostinato on its own.

• Practise performing the untuned ostinato with the song.

• Ensure that the children can confidently perform the song with the tuned ostinato accompaniment.

• Perform the untuned ostinato part, the tuned ostinato part and the song simultaneously.

Because there are three parts being performed at once, be sure that you are very familiar with all of them. You may like to appoint a musical child to lead each group. The leaders should face their groups, but should also be aware of the other groups. Remind the children that when performing, they are all pieces in a musical jigsaw that must fit together neatly.

Additional parts
A sailor went to sea (page 34) and *Old MacDonald had a glockenspiel* (page 36) contain extra tuned percussion parts to add some more variety to your performance. It is advisable to practise these parts separately before adding them to your performance.

Adding recorders to your performance
Recorder players can play the ostinatos for most of these songs. More experienced players can perform the tunes of the songs. These can be found on pages 60-63.

Rounds
A round is a song which fits with itself when sung by at least two people beginning at different times. *Wallabies and wombats* (page 26), *Bonfire's burning* (page 28), *Push, push, push your bike* (page 30) and *Kookaburra* (page 32) can all be sung as rounds, with the ostinato accompaniment. The ostinato can be played as an introduction and be continued as the children sing; alternatively the ostinato accompaniment can begin with the first group of singers. For an effective ending, the ostinato accompaniment should end when the final group of singers finish the song.

Eucalyptus, eucalyptus,

Kangaroo, kangaroo,

Wallabies and wombats,

wallabies and wombats,

Possums too, possums too.

This is sung to the tune of *Frère Jacques*. The children play a tuned ostinato, *Possums too*, (learned through actions which reflect the high and low notes) and an untuned ostinato, *Wallabies and wombats*.

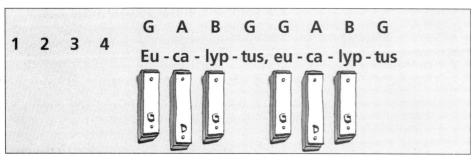

1	2	3	4	G	A	B	G		G	A	B	G

Eu - ca - lyp - tus, eu - ca - lyp - tus

You will need:
• these notes
• some untuned percussion instruments.

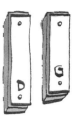

Tuned ostinato, *Possums too*

1. Perform the action pattern which matches the last line of the song.

Tap shoulders on *Pos-*; tap knees on *-sums*; tap shoulders again on *too*.

The children repeat this action pattern over and over again as they repeat the words of the last line of the song.

2. Sing the song with the action pattern.

Divide the children into two groups; one sings the song while the other repeats the action pattern. Swap roles so that everyone has the opportunity both to sing and perform the actions.

3. Now play the tuned ostinato, Possums too.

The children substitute the note **G**, played with the right hand, for each shoulder tap and **D**, played with the left hand, for each knee tap.

4. Perform the song with the Possums too ostinato.

A group of children play the ostinato while the others sing the song.

Untuned ostinato, *Wallabies and wombats*

5. Play the untuned ostinato.

A small group of children can play the rhythm of the words *Wallabies and wombats* throughout.

6. Perform the song with both ostinatos.

Divide the children into three groups: one to sing, one to play the tuned ostinato and one to play the untuned ostinato.

Action pattern

Pos - sums   too   (rest)

Tuned ostinato

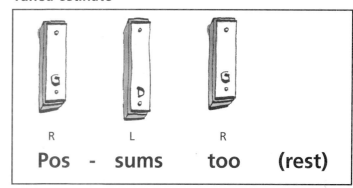

R   L   R

Pos - sums   too   (rest)

Untuned ostinato

Wal - la - bies and wom - bats

This material is photocopiable for the teaching purposes specified in this book.

Bonfire's burning, bonfire's burning,

Flames are leaping, flames are leaping,

Stand back, stand back,

Fan the fire, fan the fire.

This is sung to the tune of *London's burning*. The children play a tuned ostinato, *Bonfire's burning*, (learned through actions which reflect the high and low notes) and an untuned ostinato, *Stand back*.

You will need:
• these notes
• some untuned percussion instruments.

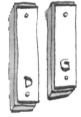

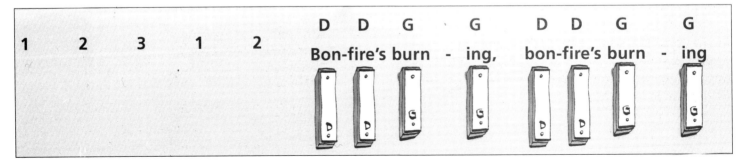

1		2		3	1		2	D	D	G		G		D	D	G		G
								Bon-fire's burn		-		ing,		bon-fire's burn		-		ing

Tuned ostinato, *Bonfire's burning*

1. Perform the action pattern which matches the first line of the song.

Tap knees on *bon-* and *-fire's*; clap hands on *burn-* and *-ing*.

The children repeat this action pattern over and over again as they repeat the words of the first line of the song.

2. Sing the song with the action pattern.

Divide the children into two groups; one sings the song while the other repeats the action pattern. Swap roles so that everyone has the opportunity both to sing and perform the actions.

3. Now play the tuned ostinato, Bonfire's burning.

The children substitute the note **D**, played with the left hand, for each knee tap and **G**, played with the right hand, for each clap.

4. Perform the song with the Bonfire's burning ostinato.

A group of children play the ostinato while the others sing the song.

Untuned ostinato, *Stand back*

5. Play the untuned ostinato.

A small group of children can play the rhythm of the words *Stand back* throughout.

6. Perform the song with both ostinatos.

Divide the children into three groups: one to sing, one to play the tuned ostinato and one to play the untuned ostinato.

Action pattern

Bon - fire's burn - ing

Tuned ostinato

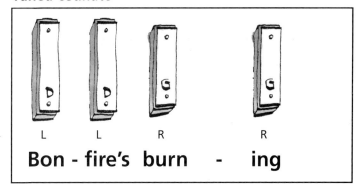

L   L   R   R

Bon - fire's burn - ing

Untuned ostinato

Stand   back,   (rest)

Push, push, push your bike,

Slowly up the hill.

Pedalling, pedalling, pedalling, pedalling

Down the hill is brill.

The children play a tuned ostinato, *Pedalling, pedalling, pedalling, pedalling,* (learned through actions which reflect the high and low notes) and an untuned ostinato, *Push, push, push your bike.*

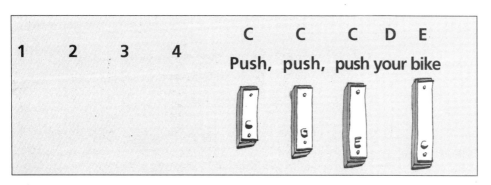

1	2	3	4	C	C	C	D	E
				Push,	push,	push	your	bike

You will need:
• these notes
• some untuned percussion instruments.

Tuned ostinato, *Pedalling, pedalling, pedalling, pedalling*

1. Repeat over and over again the action pattern which is easily learnt with the third line of the song.
Tap head **once** on the first *Pedalling*; tap shoulders **once** on the second *pedalling*; tap tummy **once** on the third *pedalling*; tap knees **once** on the fourth *pedalling*.

2. Sing the song with the action pattern.
Divide the children into two groups; one sings the song while the other repeats the action pattern. The children then swap roles.

3. Now play the tuned ostinato, Pedalling, pedalling, pedalling, pedalling.
The children substitute the note **C'** (played with the right hand) for the head tap, **G** (right hand) for the shoulder tap, **E** (left hand) for the tummy tap and **C** (left hand) for the knee tap.

4. Perform the song with the Pedalling, pedalling, pedalling, pedalling ostinato.
A group of children play the ostinato while the others sing the song.

Untuned ostinato, *Push, push, push your bike*

5. Play the untuned ostinato.
A small group of children can play the rhythm *Push, push, push your bike* throughout.

6. Perform the song with both ostinatos.
Divide the children into three groups: one to sing and one to play each ostinato.

Action pattern

Pedalling, pedalling, pedalling, pedalling

Tuned ostinato

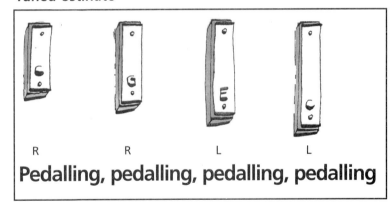

R   R   L   L

Pedalling, pedalling, pedalling, pedalling

Untuned ostinato

Push,   push,   push your bike

This material is photocopiable for the teaching purposes specified in this book.

Kookaburra sits in the old gum tree,

Merry little king of the bush is he.

Laugh, kookaburra, laugh, kookaburra,

Gay your life must be.

The children play a tuned ostinato, *Laugh, kookaburra, laugh*, (learned through actions which reflect the high and low notes) and an untuned ostinato, *Merry little king*.

You will need:
• these notes
• some untuned percussion instruments.

	A A A A B	B B A	F#	A	F#
1 2 3 4	Koo-ka-bur-ra sits	in the old	gum	tree__	

Tuned ostinato, *Laugh, kookaburra, laugh*

1. Perform the action pattern which is easily learnt with part of the third line of the song.
Tap knees once on each *laugh*; clap hands once on *kookaburra*.

The children repeat this action pattern over and over again as they repeat the words of the third line of the song.

2. Sing the song with the action pattern.
Divide the children into two groups; one sings the song while the other repeats the action pattern. The children then swap roles.

3. Now play the tuned ostinato Laugh, **kookaburra, laugh.**
The tuned ostinato involves playing two notes at once. The children substitute the notes **D** (left hand) and **F♯** (right hand), played simultaneously for the knee taps and **G** (left hand) and **B** (right hand), played simultaneously for the hand claps.

4. Perform the song with the Laugh, **kookaburra, laugh** ostinato.
A group of children play the ostinato while the others sing the song.

Untuned ostinato, *Merry little king*

5. Play the untuned ostinato pattern.
Ask a small group of children to play the rhythm of the words *Merry little king* throughout.

6. Perform the song with both ostinatos.
Divide the children into three groups: one to sing and one to play each ostinato.

Action pattern

Laugh,   kookaburra, laugh   (rest)

Tuned ostinato (pairs of notes played simultaneously)

L and R   L and R   L and R

Laugh,   kookaburra, laugh   (rest)

Untuned ostinato

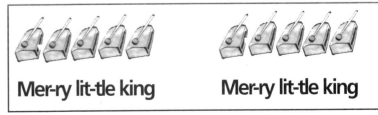

Mer-ry lit-tle king   Mer-ry lit-tle king

This material is photocopiable for the teaching purposes specified in this book.

A sailor went to sea, sea, sea,

To see what he could see, see, see.

But all that he could see, see, see,

Was the bottom of the deep blue sea, sea, sea.

The children play a tuned ostinato, *Sailor went to sea*. (This is learned with actions which accustom the children to the beater pattern they will use later.) The children also play a tuned part, *Sea, sea, sea*.

You will need:
• these notes
for the ostinato

• these notes
for the tuned
part.

1	2	3	A (4) A	D' sai -	A lor	B went	A to	F# sea,	A sea,	A sea

Tuned ostinato, *Sailor went to sea*

1. Perform the action pattern which matches the first line of the song.

Tap left knee on *sai-* and *went*; tap right knee on *-lor* and *to*; clap hands on *sea*.

The children repeat this action pattern over and over again as they repeat the first line.

2. Sing the song with the action pattern.

Divide the children into two groups; one sings the song while the other repeats the action pattern throughout. Notice that the song begins after three counts but that the actions begin after four.

3. Now play the tuned ostinato, *Sailor went to sea*.

The children play the notes **A**, and **D** with the left hand, and **A** with the right hand.

4. Perform the song with the *Sailor went to sea ostinato.*

A group of children play the ostinato while the others sing the song.

Tuned part, *Sea, sea, sea*

5. Play the tuned part.

The children choose any number and combination of the notes **F#**, **A** and **D'** and play them whenever the words *sea* or *see* are sung.

6. Perform the song with the tuned ostinato and tuned part.

Divide the children into three groups: one to sing, one to play the tuned ostinato and one to play the tuned part. Notice that the tuned part and the ostinato overlap on the first *sea* or *see* of each line.

Action pattern

Sai - lor went to sea

Tuned ostinato

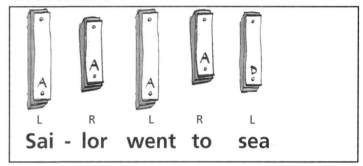

Sai - lor went to sea

Tuned part

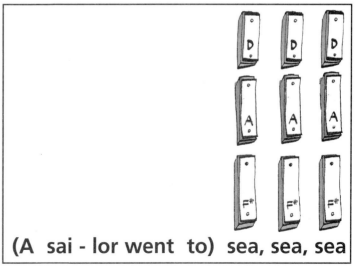

(A sai - lor went to) sea, sea, sea

This material is photocopiable for the teaching purposes specified in this book.

Swing low, sweet chariot,

Coming for to carry me home.

Swing low, sweet chariot,

Coming for to carry me home.

You will need:
• these notes
• some untuned percussion instruments.

The children play a tuned ostinato, *Coming for to carry me.* (This is learned with actions which accustom the children to the beater pattern they will use later.) The children also play an untuned ostinato *Swing low, sweet.*

1	2	3	4	A	F		A	F	F D C
				Swing low,			sweet cha	-	ri-ot_

OSTINATO ACCOMPANIMENTS

Tuned ostinato, *Coming for to carry me*

1. Perform the action pattern which is easily learnt with part of the second line of the song.

Tap right hand on right knee on *com-*; tap left hand on left knee on *for*; cross over to tap right hand on left knee on *car-*; tap left hand on left knee on *me*.

The children repeat the action pattern over and over again as they say the words.

2. Sing the song with the action pattern.

Divide the children into two groups; one sings the song while the other performs the action pattern seven times and the ending pattern once: right hand on right knee, left hand on left knee, right hand on right knee.

***3. Now play the tuned ostinato,* Coming for to carry me.**

The children play the note **F** with the right hand, **C** with the left hand and **D** with the right hand.

4. Learn the ending.

This consists of the notes **F C F**. Play **F** with the right hand and **C** with the left hand.

5. Perform the song with the* Coming for to carry me *ostinato.

Ask some children to play the ostinato seven times and the ending once to fit with the song.

Untuned ostinato, *Swing low, sweet*

6. Play this untuned ostinato.

A small group of children can play the rhythm of the words *Swing low, sweet* throughout.

7. Perform the song with both ostinatos.

Divide the children into three groups: one to sing and one to play each ostinato.

Action pattern

Com-ing for to car - ry me

Tuned ostinato

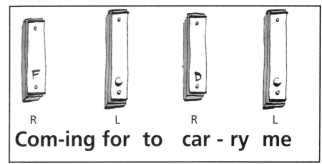

Com-ing for to car - ry me

Ending

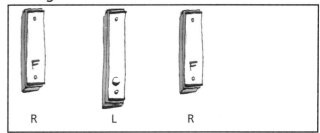

Untuned ostinato

Swing low, sweet

This material is photocopiable for the teaching purposes specified in this book.

My brother did-a tell me that you go mango walk,

You go mango walk, you go mango walk.

My brother did-a tell me that you go mango walk,

And steal all the number 'leven.

The children play a tuned ostinato, *Go mango walk, and steal all the number.* (This is learned with actions which accustom the children to the beater pattern they will use later.) The children also play an untuned ostinato, *'leven.*

You will need:
• these notes
• some untuned percussion instruments.

1	2	3	D' (4) My	D' bro-ther	E' did	D' a-tell	C' me	B that	C' you	B go	A man	G	B - go	D walk,	G	B You

Tuned ostinato, *Go mango walk, and steal all the number*

1. Repeat over and over again the action pattern which matches part of the third and fourth lines of the song.
Tap left leg with left hand and right leg with right hand: left right right left right on *Go man-go walk and*. Repeat this pattern, crossing over with left hand to tap right leg on *steal all the num-ber*.

2. Sing the song with the action pattern.
Divide the children into two groups; one sings the song while the other performs the action pattern four times, missing out the final right tap the last time. Notice that the actions begin after four counts.

3. Now play the tuned ostinato pattern Go mango walk, and steal all the number.
The children play the note **D** with the left hand, **D'** with the right hand and **G** with the left hand.

4. Learn the ending.
To play the ending, leave out the final **D'**.

5. Perform the song with the Go mango walk, and steal all the number *ostinato*.
Ask some children to play the ostinato three times and the ending once to fit with the song.

Untuned ostinato, *'leven*

6. Play this untuned ostinato.
Ask a small group of children to play the rhythm of *'leven* on untuned percussion throughout the song.

7. Perform the song with both ostinatos.
Divide the children into three groups: one to sing and one to play each ostinato.

Action pattern

Tuned ostinato

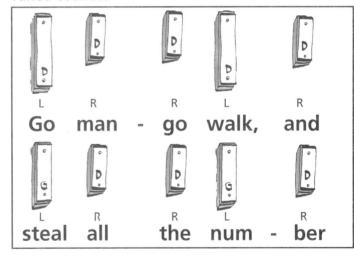

Untuned ostinato

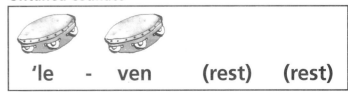

Old MacDonald had a glockenspiel

Old MacDonald had a glock, B B A A G.

On that glock he had some Gs, B B A A G.

With a G G here, and a G G there,

Here a G, there a G, everywhere a G G,

Old MacDonald had a glock, B B A A G.

This is sung to the tune of *Old MacDonald had a farm*. The children play a tuned ostinato, *Old MacDonald had a glock*. (This is learned with actions which accustom the children to the beater pattern they will use later.) The children also play a tuned part, *B B A A G* and an improvised part, *With a G G here*.

You will need:
• these notes for the tuned ostinato part

• these notes for the tuned part

• this note for the improvised part.

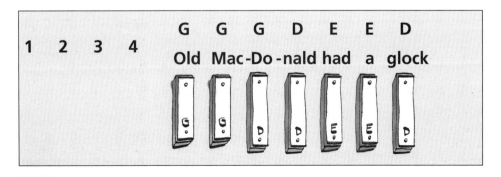

Tuned ostinato, *Old MacDonald had a glock*

1. Perform the action pattern over and over again while repeating the words of the first line.
Tap right hand twice on right knee; left hand twice on left knee; cross over for right hand twice on left knee; left hand once on left knee.

2. Sing the song with the action pattern.
Divide the children into two groups; one sings the song while the other performs the action pattern seven times and the ending once: tap right hand on right knee twice, left hand on left knee twice and right hand on right knee three times.

3. Now play the tuned ostinato, Old MacDonald had a glock.
The children play the notes **G** and **E** with the right hand and **D** with the left hand.

4. Learn the ending.
This consists of the notes **G G D D G G G**. Play **G** with the right hand and **D** with the left hand.

5. Perform the song with the tuned ostinato.
Ask some children to play the ostinato seven times and the ending once to fit with the song.

Two additional parts: *B B A A G* and *With a G G here.*

6. Play the tuned part **B B A A G**.
A group of children can play the notes **B B A A G** as the letters are sung.

7. Play the improvised part, **With a G G here**
A small group of children can improvise rhythms on the note **G** during the third and fourth lines. The children must stop at the end of the fourth line.

Action pattern

Old Mac-Do - nald had a glock

Tuned ostinato

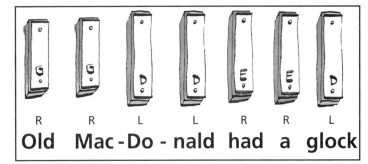

R R L L R R L
Old Mac-Do - nald had a glock

Ending

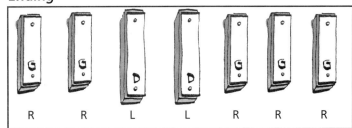

R R L L R R R

Tuned part

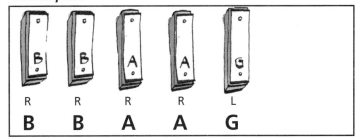

R R R R L
B B A A G

This material is photocopiable for the teaching purposes specified in this book.

Pentatonic scales

What is a pentatonic scale?

The word pentatonic is derived from the Greek *penta* meaning five and *tonos* meaning tone. A pentatonic scale has five note names in it. The five notes are a fixed combination of notes determined by the starting note of the scale.

High and low notes

Each pentatonic scale is made up of five notes. On some tuned percussion instruments, you may find that you have two of a note – a high one and a low one. You can use both the high and the low notes for most of the pentatonic scale activities, and, if you wish, you can combine two different-sized instruments to give you more notes.

The notes of the pentatonic scale starting on F are *F G A C D.*

The notes of the pentatonic scale starting on C are *C D E G A.*

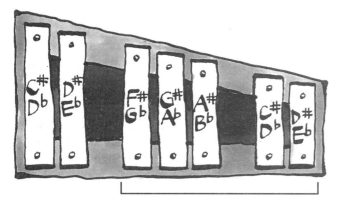

The notes of the pentatonic scale starting on F♯ are *F♯ G♯ A♯ C♯ D♯ (which many also be written as G♭ A♭ B♭ D♭ E♭).*

The notes of the pentatonic scale starting on G are *G A B D E.*

Making up music using the pentatonic scale

All the activities in this section involve the children in making up their own music. The pentatonic scale is an excellent base to use for this because of its versatility and simplicity, and because the combination of notes in the pentatonic scale sound well with each other.

Each activity consists of a simple process for the children to go through in order to make up their own music. On the accompanying recording, example musical ideas are given. These are intended to be indications of what might result from going through these processes. Be aware that when making up music, there are no right or wrong musical ideas, though some may be more effective or more appropriate than others.

Adding recorders to performances

If you want to include recorders in any of the activities in this section, it is advisable where possible to use the pentatonic scale of **G** (notes **G A B D E**), which is the easiest to play on the recorder.

Points on performance and appraisal

First and foremost, encourage the children to enjoy their music-making and to develop the means and confidence to perform independently of your help. When they are performing without you, encourage your children to:
• have their beaters poised over their starting note ready to begin
• to begin together at an agreed signal or count in
• to keep time together by listening carefully to each other
When appraising your children's work, commend them not only on content, but on presentation and organisation as well.

Which notes are these?

? ? ? ?

Which notes are these?

Can you tell me which they are?

This song is sung to the tune of *Who built the ark?* A child makes up a four-note tune to take the place of the second line. The other children identify its notes by listening.

You will need:
• an instrument with the notes of the pentatonic scale of **F**.

1	2	3	4	F	F		D	C
				Which notes			are these?	

The activity

1. The children sing the song.
For the second line of the song, ask the children to clap four times with the beat of the song.

2. Choose one child to play the instrument.
The child chooses two notes on the instrument and plays them to the other children. (S)he names them and describes the sounds.

3. The child makes up a four-note tune out of the two chosen notes.
Place the instrument where it can't be seen by the other children. The children sing the song and the player performs a four-note tune during the second line, playing one note for each of the four claps.

4. The children name the notes.
After listening, the children name the order in which the notes were played.

Variation
• Increase the number of notes that can be played to three or four.

Words and phrases that can be repeated many times

DINNER'S READY

red, orange, yellow, green, blue, indigo, violet

Turn the T.V. off

William Shakespeare

1815 - Battle of Waterloo

RING, RING! WHO'S THERE? HOLD ON! - GOODBYE

An example plan for a piece of music

Begin quietly
get louder
then quieter
end quietly
perform the ostinato eight times
1 2 3 4 5 6 7 8

Improvising (or making up music on the spot) using the pentatonic scale always sounds good, whatever is played, as it's impossible to make a mistake! In this activity, several children play an ostinato while one child improvises a tune using the pentatonic scale. Before doing this, the children make up a vocal, or spoken, ostinato and improvise using words or phrases.

You will need:
• at least two instruments with the notes of the same pentatonic scale. (See page 42.) The instrument below shows the notes of the pentatonic scale of C.

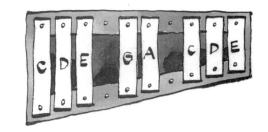

C D E G A C D E

The activity

1. The children make up a vocal, or spoken, ostinato using words or phrases.

The children repeat a simple phrase over and over again. This is the ostinato.

2. The children make a plan for an ostinato accompaniment.

The children decide how many times to repeat the vocal ostinato, and how loudly or quietly to perform.

3. Some children improvise while the ostinato is performed.

Divide the children into two groups. One performs the ostinato. The children in the other group improvise using words or fragments of the ostinato, speaking, whispering or singing them in any way they like. They listen to the ostinato in order to finish at the same time.

4. The children play an ostinato on the tuned instruments.

The children make up a tune for the ostinato phrase and perform it according to the plan made earlier for the ostinato accompaniment.

5. A child improvises on a tuned instrument while the ostinato is performed.

Choose a child to improvise on a tuned instrument while the other children perform the ostinato part. The child listens to the ostinato as (s)he performs and finishes at the same time.

Variation

• Play the rhythm of the ostinato on untuned percussion instruments, such as drums or claves.

Din-ner's rea-dy

I can play my own tune,
I can play my own tune,
Listen to how it goes
I will play it now.

In this activity, a short sung (or spoken) section (A) is alternated with tunes made up by the children (B, C, D, E and so on.)

The order in which the sections are performed is ABACADA... which in music is called rondo form.

(The song melody is given at the back of this book and on the recording.)

You will need:
• at least two instruments with the notes of the same pentatonic scale. This instrument shows the notes of the pentatonic scale of **F#**, but you can use any of the sample scales on page 42.

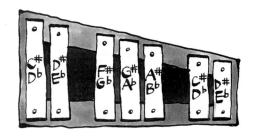

1	2	3	4	C# D# F# G# A#	F#
				(D♭ E♭ G♭ A♭ B♭	G♭)
				I can play my own	tune

The activity

1. Perform the song.

Alternate singing the words (or chanting them if you prefer) with whispering them. Don't pause between the sung and whispered sections.

2. Improvise a rhythm while the words are whispered.

One or two children make up rhythms during the whispered sections. They can use voices, body percussion, or untuned percussion, and should finish performing when the whispered section ends.

3. Use a tuned percussion instrument to improvise a tune while the words are whispered.

One or two children make up tunes during the whispered sections. The children finish performing their tunes when the whispered section ends.

Take turns so that everyone has the chance to make up a tune.

Variation

• Some children can play the rhythm of the words during the sung (or spoken) sections on untuned percussion instruments such as tambourines or woodblocks.

What's today? Monday.
What's on? Back to school.
  On to the next day.

What's today? Tuesday.
What's on? Swimming.
  On to the next day.

What's today? Wednesday.
What's on? Basketball.
  On to the next day.

What's today? Thursday.
What's on? Music.
  On to the next day ...

What's today? Sunday.
What's on? Go to the cinema.
  (Last time) No more days.

Using the activities of their week, the children make up a 'question and answer' piece of music. The questions have fixed tunes; however the answers are improvised and therefore sound different each time.

You will need:
• instruments with the notes of any pentatonic scales. (See page 42.) The instrument below shows the notes of the pentatonic scale of **F**.

1	2	3	4	●	●	●	●
				What's	to-day?	Mon -	day

The activity

1. Discuss the activities your children are involved in during the week.

Some hobbies and activities take place on specific days. Organise the children into pairs, delegating a day to each pair for which they will think of one activity.

2. Perform your version of What's today?

If possible, the children sit in a circle in the order of their days. Everyone chants *What's today?* and *What's on?*, and *On to the next day*. Each pair of children names its respective day and hobby or activity for that day. (The chant opposite contains examples.)

3. Replace the words with body percussion sounds matching the rhythm.

Make up a body percussion pattern for each of the two questions. Each pair of children makes up a body percussion pattern for its chosen day and activity.

4. Replace the body percussion sounds with tunes.

Use the code to translate the body percussion patterns into tunes for the questions.

Organise the children to play the fixed questions and answers to make a piece. The lines *On to the next day* and *No more days* are always spoken.

Code

Clap = **C**

Stamp = **D**

Finger click = **F**

Mouth pop = **G**

Chest thump = **A**

Any action not mentioned = **C'**

This material is photocopiable for the teaching purposes specified in this book.

C How many spots on a spotty dalmatian?

R *Secrets of the animal kingdom.*

C How much does a kingfisher weigh?

R *Secrets of the animal kingdom.*

C What does a baby armadillo eat?

R *Secrets of the animal kingdom.*

C Do whales sleep?

R *Secrets of the animal kingdom.*

The children make up a call and response (or question and answer) piece. The call should be different each time, but the response is always the same.

You will need:
• at least two instruments with the notes of the same pentatonic scale. (See page 42.) The instrument below shows the notes of the pentatonic scale of **G**.

1	2	3	4	

How ma-ny spots on a spot-ty dal-ma-tian

The activity

1. Introduce call and response.

Perform the call and response given. Choose individual children to perform each call; the rest of the children reply with the response, which is always the same.

Encourage the children to make up different calls.

2. The children substitute body percussion sounds for the words.

The children replace the words of the call and response with claps, taps, clicks and other body percussion sounds. They perform one sound for each syllable and match the rhythm of the words. Everyone should perform the same fixed sequence of sounds for the response. Each call can be a different sequence of sounds.

Keep a steady pulse going throughout and begin each new call without a break.

3. The children substitute instruments for the body percussion.

The children replace the body percussion sounds with tunes or rhythms played on tuned or untuned instruments, or a mixture. Agree on a fixed rhythm or tune for the response and make up different ones for the call.

Variations

• Ask the children to make up new call and response chants on subjects such as different places in the world, famous people, or sport.
• Make up a call and response piece out of tunes or rhythms without using words as a starting point.

A   **Wellington boots,**
A   **Wellington boots,**
B   **Muddy puddle,**
A   **Wellington boots.**

A   **London, Paris, Washington, Rome,**
A   **London, Paris, Washington, Rome,**
B   **Capital cities of the world,**
A   **London, Paris, Washington, Rome.**

A   **Six sevens are forty-two,**
A   **Six sevens are forty-two,**
B   **Ten nines are ninety,**
A   **Six sevens are forty-two.**

A   **Yellow and blue,**
A   **Yellow and blue,**
B   **Together they're green,**
A   **Yellow and blue.**

The children make up a short piece out of two musical phrases: A (apple) and B (blackberry). The phrases are organised into the structure AABA (apple, apple, blackberry, apple). This is a common structure in music; *Hot cross buns* follows this structure.

You will need:
• some instruments with the notes of the same pentatonic scale. (See page 42.) The instrument below shows the notes of the pentatonic scale of **C**.

The activity

1. Select a topic.
Choose a subject, such as food, articles of clothing, famous personalities, schoolwork-related ideas, and so on, for which the children can think of two phrases.

2. Divide the children into pairs.
Each pair thinks of two phrases. The phrases should be of a similar length and have contrasting rhythms.

3. The children make an AABA speech rhyme out of their phrases.
Each pair decides which of its phrases is phrase A and which phrase B. It then builds a speech rhyme following the structure AABA.

Encourage the children to say their phrases with enthusiasm and a strong rhythm!

4. The children make up two tunes, one for each phrase.
The tunes should fit the rhythms of the phrases (one note for each syllable). Encourage the children to use all available notes if they wish, or to repeat notes or play more than one at a time. The tunes can either be memorised or written down.

5. Make an AABA piece of music out of the two tunes.
The children play their musical phrases in the AABA structure to make a piece of music. Give them the opportunity to perform them to the other children. Because the pieces will be short, the children can perform them twice, if they wish.

Knock, knock!

D　G
Knock knock!

E'　D'
Who's　there?

E E D
I-sa-bel.

E' E' E'　D'
I-sa-bel who?

D E G A A A A B A G G G
I-sa-bel ne-ces-sa-ry on a bi-cy-cle?!

Using the notes in any pentatonic scale, children set a *Knock, knock!* joke to music.

You will need:
• at least one instrument with the notes of a pentatonic scale for each group in the class. (See page 42.) The instrument below shows the notes of the pentatonic scale of **G**.

(The example joke given shows both the question and answer played on tuned percussion. If you have limited resources of tuned percussion instruments, you can use a mixture of tuned and untuned percussion instead.)

The activity

1. Divide the children into pairs or groups.

Each pair or group requires at least two untuned percussion instruments, one tuned instrument and a *Knock, knock!* joke.

2. The children play the knock knock! *joke on untuned percussion.*

The children play the rhythm of the words on untuned percussion instruments. Encourage them to perform it as a conversation, taking turns to say each line of the joke.

3. Discuss ways to make up tunes.

In their tunes, the children can consider using:
- repeated notes *(see Twinkle, twinkle);*
- notes moving by step (notes which are next to each other) *(see Frère Jacques);*
- notes grouped to fit with the flow of the words *(see Row, row, row your boat).*

4. The children make up pentatonic tunes on tuned instruments to fit the rhythm of the words of their Knock, knock! *jokes.*

If necessary to give everyone a turn to play, delegate different lines of the joke to tuned and untuned instruments. If appropriate, use instruments imaginatively. For instance, at the end of the *Isabel* joke, ring a bell quietly before simulating a crash, to prove that a bell is necessary on a bicycle!

5. Each group performs its piece.

Ask the children to present their spoken joke first and then their instrumental piece. Because the pieces will be short, the children can perform them twice if they wish.

Examples of tunes

The beginning of *Twinkle, twinkle little star* contains repeated notes.

Twin - kle, twin - kle lit - tle star

The beginning of *Frère Jacques* contains notes moving by step.

Frè - re Jac - ques, Frè - re Jac - ques

The *Merrily, merrily ...* line of *Row, row, row your boat* contains notes grouped to fit with the flow of the words.

Mer - ri - ly, mer - ri - ly, mer - ri - ly, mer - ri - ly

Don't slip
On the grass
With a glass.
You'll trip,
Glass'll smash,
Hear the crash.

Using the notes of the pentatonic scale, the children set a short poem to music.

You will need:
• photocopies of the poems
• at least one instrument with the notes of a pentatonic scale for each group in the class. (See page 42.) The instrument below shows the notes of the pentatonic scale of **F**.

A rabbit raced a turtle,
You know the turtle won;
And Mister Bunny came in late,
A little hot cross bun!

My cat has swallowed a bird
And if you tickle her feet
It's not a purr that's heard
But a sweet 'tweet tweet tweet tweet'.

A balloon is nice
And so is a pin
But it's gone in a trice
If you stick the pin in.

The activity

1. Divide the children into groups of four or five.
Each group chooses a poem. Give out photocopies of the poems for reference.

2. Each group explores its chosen poem.
The children recite their poems and list features which suggest sounds.

3. Discuss the qualities that each sound associated with the poem might have.
Are the sounds loud or quiet? Fast or slow? Gentle or abrasive? Long or short? High or low?

4. Each group makes up a poem accompaniment using untuned instruments.
The children choose instruments that reflect the sounds associated with the poems. They perform the sounds as they recite their poems.

5. The groups make up tunes to fit with the words of the poems.
In their tunes, the children can consider using:
• repeated notes;
• notes moving by step (notes which are next to each other);
• notes grouped to fit with the flow of the words.
Explore these possibilities with the children, using the tunes on page 57.

6. Each group performs its final piece.
The children put the words, tune and accompaniment together and present it as a performance. They can recite their poem first and then play the instrumental piece. Short pieces can be performed twice.

Features of poems suggesting sounds

footsteps
short, regular sounds, eg. a two-tone woodblock playing a steady beat

tripping over
a dull, thudding sound, eg. a flat palm hitting a tambour.

smashing and crashing
long, high sounds, eg. a cascade of metal instruments such as Indian bells and triangles.

Don't slip on the grass

With a glass...

Melody lines

Buns cross hot - Hot cross buns

Page 10, Track 2

High, low, middle. High, low, middle. Change the or - der of the notes from High, low, middle.

Wallabies and wombats - Frère Jacques

Page 26, Track 9

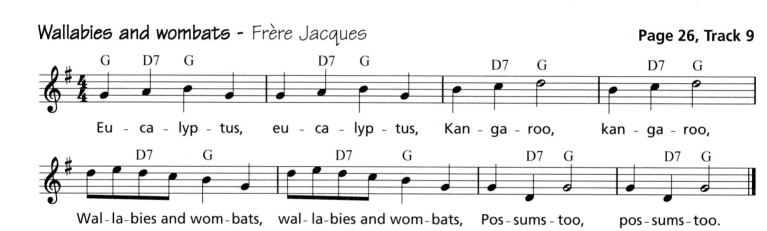

Eu - ca - lyp - tus, eu - ca - lyp - tus, Kan - ga - roo, kan - ga - roo,

Wal - la - bies and wom - bats, wal - la - bies and wom - bats, Pos - sums - too, pos - sums - too.

Bonfire's burning - London's burning

Page 28, Track 10

Bon - fire's burn - ing, bon - fire's burn - ing, Flames are leap - ing, flames are leap - ing, Stand

back, stand back, Fan the fi - re, fan the fi - re.

Melody lines

Push, push, push your bike - *Row, row, row your boat* **Page 30, Track 11**

Push, push, push your bike, Slow - ly up the hill.

Pe - dal - ling, pe - dal - ling, pe - dal - ling, pe - dal - ling Down a - gain is brill.

Kookaburra **Page 32, Track 12**

Koo - ka - bur - ra sits in the old gum tree, ___ Mer - ry lit - tle king of the

bush is he, ___ Laugh, koo - ka - bur - ra, laugh, koo - ka - bur - ra, Gay your life must be.

A sailor went to sea **Page 34, Track 13**

A sai - lor went to sea, sea, sea, To see what he could see, see, see, But

all that he could see, see, see, Was the bot - tom of the deep blue sea, sea, sea.

Melody lines

Swing low, sweet chariot

Page 36, Track 14

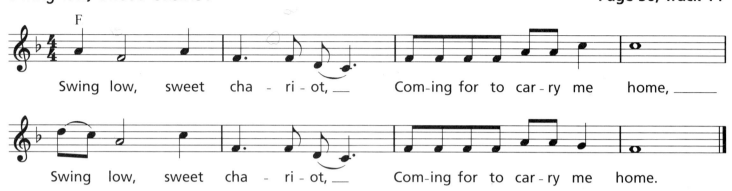

Swing low, sweet cha - ri - ot, — Com-ing for to car - ry me home, ——

Swing low, sweet cha - ri - ot, — Com-ing for to car - ry me home.

Mango walk

Page 38, Track 15

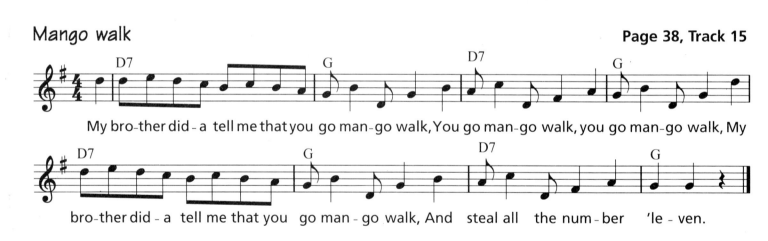

My bro-ther did - a tell me that you go man-go walk, You go man-go walk, you go man-go walk, My

bro-ther did - a tell me that you go man - go walk, And steal all the num - ber 'le - ven.

Old MacDonald had a glockenspiel - *Old MacDonald had a farm*

Page 40, Track 16

Old Mac-Don-ald had a glock, B B A A G. On that glock he had some Gs,

Melody lines

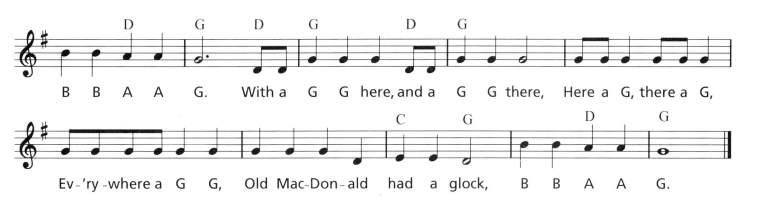

D	G	D	G	D	G

B B A A G. With a G G here, and a G G there, Here a G, there a G,

		C	G	D	G

Ev-'ry-where a G G, Old Mac-Don-ald had a glock, B B A A G.

Which notes are these - *Who built the ark?*

Page 44, Track 17

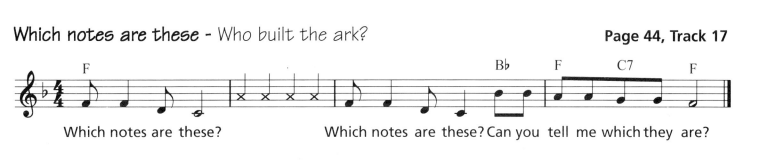

Which notes are these?   Which notes are these? Can you tell me which they are?

My own tune

Page 48, Track 19

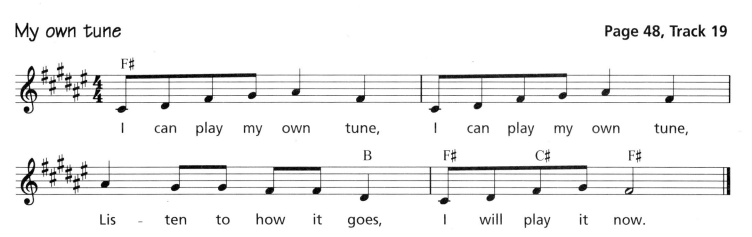

I can play my own tune, I can play my own tune,

Lis - ten to how it goes, I will play it now.

Glossary and acknowledgements

Accidental
A note with a flat or sharp in its name, eg. B♭, G♯.

Accompaniment
Music which supports the main instrumental or vocal line, e.g. the piano music or percussion part which is played while someone sings a song.

Alto
Middle range in pitch – see page 6.

Bass
Low range in pitch – see page 6.

Chime bars
A type of tuned percussion instrument – see page 6.

Chord
A group of two or more notes played together.

Flat
The musical sign ♭, which slightly lowers the note it refers to. When flattened, E is lowered to E♭.

Glockenspiel
A type of tuned percussion instrument – see page 6.

Improvise
To create music instantaneously. An improvisation is a piece of music which is made up as it is performed.

Metallophone
A type of tuned percussion instrument – see page 6.

Ostinato
A repeating pattern of notes – see page 24.

Pentatonic scale
A combination of pitches – see page 42.

Pitch
High sounds, low sounds and all in between.

Rhythm
The grouping of short sounds, long sounds and silences.

Rhythmic pulse
A regular beat, (sometimes heard but usually felt) similar to the steady tap of walking feet or the tick of a clock.

Sharp
The musical sign ♯, which raises slightly the note it refers to. When sharpened, C is raised to C♯.

Soprano
High range in pitch – see page 6.

Tuned percussion
A family of pitched instruments - see page 6.

Untuned ostinato
An accompaniment consisting of a repeated rhythmic pattern played on an untuned instrument e.g. a tambourine or claves.

Xylophone
A type of tuned percussion instrument – see page 6.

The author and publishers would like to thank the following copyright holders and contributors:

Dot Fraser for **My own tune** © 1996 Dot Fraser

Carrie Morrow for the original ideas from which **Tea time** and **Adding accidentals** were developed © 1996 Carrie Morrow

Sue Nicholls for **High, middle, low** © 1996 Sue Nicholls

Ana Sanderson for the original idea for **Knock, knock!**

Allan Watson for the poems in *From poem to song* **My cat has swallowed a bird** and **A balloon is nice** © 1996 Allan Watson

For their help in the preparation of this book the author and publishers would like to thank Lynne Jackson, Theresa Kelly, Lis McCullogh, Lynn Packer, Linda Read, Sheena Roberts, Ana Sanderson, Edwina Sharp, Marie Tomlinson, Allan Watson, and the children of Malden Manor School, Surrey.

Every effort has been made to trace and acknowledge copyright owners. If any right has been omitted, the publishers offer their apologies and will rectify this in subsequent editions following notification.